COOKING WITH

Illustrations by Albert Uderzo

Recipes by Marie-Christine Crabos

ℛ
RAVETTE BOOKS

Dear Asterix fan,

I hope that this book will give you many hours of fun in the kitchen and at the table, where you will be able to astound your friends and family with your culinary expertise.

Some of the ingredients are typically French and well worth searching out, so that you may obtain that true 'Asterix' taste in your cooking.

Bon Appetit!

Printed and bound in Italy for Ravette Books Limited,
3 Glenside Estate, Star Road, Partridge Green,
Horsham, West Sussex RH13 8RA
An Egmont Company

ISBN 1 85304 455 5

CONTENTS

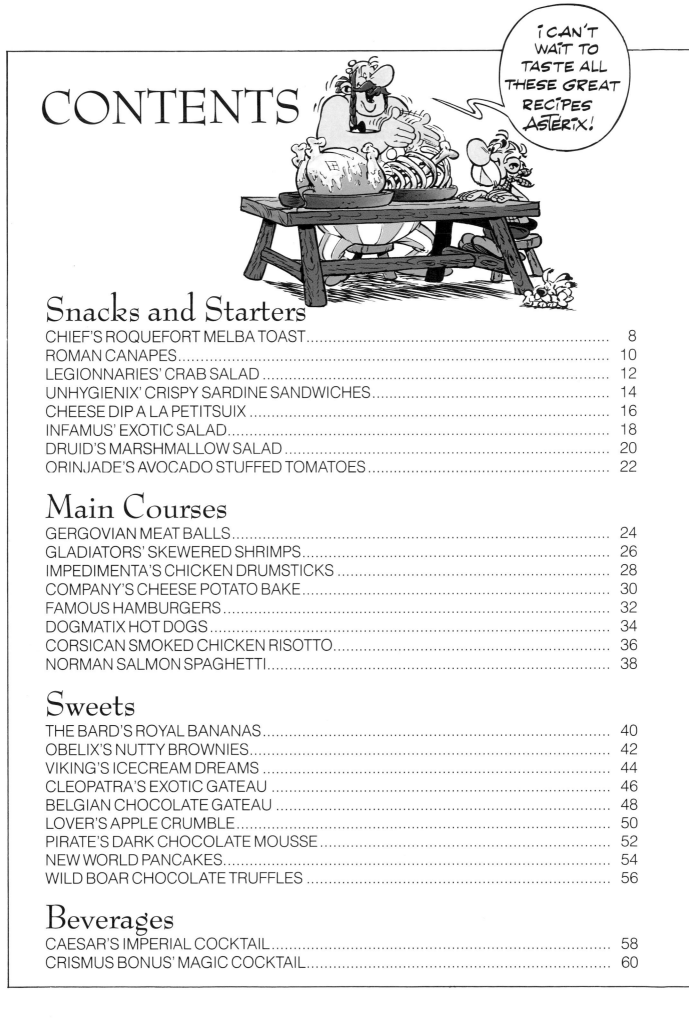

I CAN'T WAIT TO TASTE ALL THESE GREAT RECIPES ASTERIX!

Snacks and Starters

Main Courses

Sweets

Beverages

CHIEF'S ROQUEFORT MELBA TOAST

SERVES 4
Preparation: 10mins **Cooking** 15mins
Equipment: a large bowl, grater, knife for buttering, baking tray, spatula, fork, serving dish.
Preheat oven: Gas 2 (150°C)

I'LL CUT THE CHEESE. YOU BRING THE MELBA TOASTS OBELIX.

INGREDIENTS

8 Crisp bakes or toasts Francais

4 natural petits-suisses

50g of Roquefort cheese

25g of shelled nuts

50g of softened butter

black pepper or Cayenne pepper

Put the Roquefort in the bowl and mash with a fork.

Add the 4 petits-suisses. Blend together.

Grate the nuts and add to the mixture. Mix well.

Add black pepper or Cayenne pepper to taste.

Spread the Melba toast with the softened butter. Be careful not to break them.

Place the toast on a baking tray. Cover each slice with the Roquefort mixture.

Place the baking tray in the oven Gas 2 (150°C) for approx 15 minutes.

Take the tray out of the oven. Remove the toast and arrange them on a serving dish.

ROMAN CANAPES

MAKES 24 CANAPES
Preparation: 15 mins
No cooking
Equipment: a kitchen knife,
a spoon, a buttering knife,
a board, a flat plate, a sieve,
kitchen paper, a tray
or serving dish.

A ROMAN ORGY ISN'T A ROMAN ORGY WITHOUT TIT-BITS!

INGREDIENTS

6 slices of
white bread

100g of
softened butter

2 tablespoons
mustard

6 slices
of vacuum packed
cheddar cheese

24 water-cress
leaves

6 red
radishes

Cut off all the crusts from
the bread.

With a spoon, mix together
the butter and the mustard
on the plate.

Butter the slices of bread with
the butter mixture and cut
into 4.

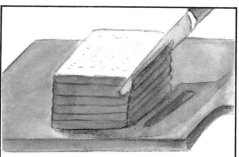

Cut the slices of cheddar into
4 and place them onto
the 24 squares of bread.

Wash and drain the cress,
wash the 6 radishes.
Dry them on kitchen paper.

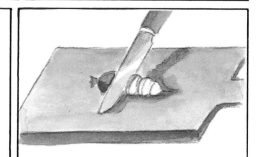

Top and tail each radish and
cut into 4 circles.

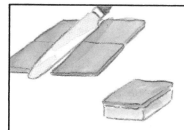

Arrange the canapes on the tray or serving plate.

On each canape, place a well-dried watercress leaf.

To finish, place a radish circle on each leaf.

11

LEGIONNAIRES' CRAB SALAD

LEGIONNARIES! FORM A CRAB!

SERVES 4
Preparation: 20 mins
Cooking: 15 mins
Equipment: small saucepan, 1 kitchen knife, 2 shallow bowls, a bowl, a salad bowl, colander.

INGREDIENTS

8 crab sticks

2 ripe avocadoes

1 lettuce

1 grapefruit

2 eggs

1 lemon

250g pot of mayonnaise

In the pan, heat the water to boiling point.

Gently place the eggs in the water and boil for 12 minutes.

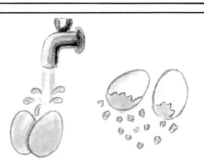
When hard-boiled, remove the shells under cold running water.

Peel the grapefruit, remove the skins from the segments and save the juice.

Skin the avocadoes and remove the stones.

Cut the avocadoes into cubes and sprinkle with lemon juice.

Wash the lettuce and shake dry. Put the lettuce in the salad bowl.

Add the grapefruit segments (without juice) and the avocadoes.

Chop the crab sticks into three and add to the salad.

Decorate the salad bowl with the 2 sliced hard boiled eggs.

Put the mayonnaise into a bowl and add the grapefruit juice.

Mix well, and pour the mayonnaise over the salad just before serving.

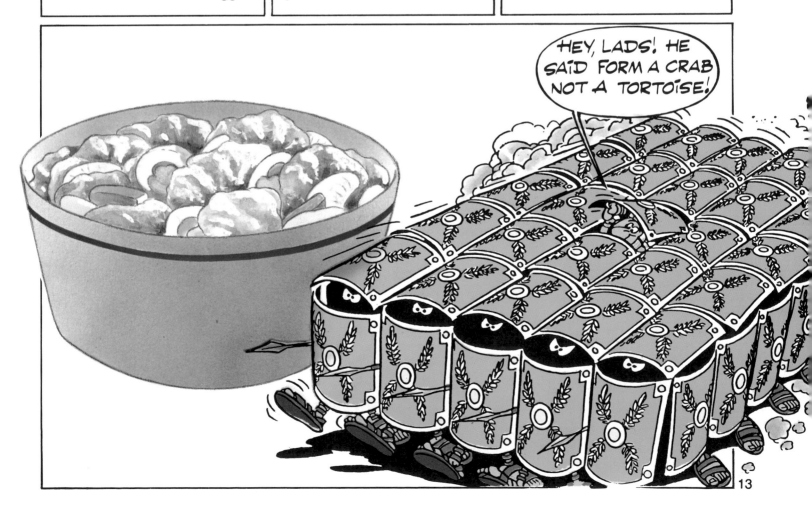

13

SERVES 4
Preparation: 15 mins
Cooking: 10 mins
Equipment: tin opener, mixing bowl, medium-sized saucepan, frying pan, fork, whisk, cup, knife.

INGREDIENTS

1 tin sardines in oil

100ml milk

1 level tbsp flour

100g grated gruyere cheese

1 egg

50g butter

1 tsp oil

salt   pepper

8 slices of bread

SARDINES ARE FOR EATING ...

Open the tin of sardines. Pour the oil into the bowl.

Remove the bones and skin from the sardines and place in the bowl.

In the saucepan, gently heat the milk.

When the milk is hot, add the cheese and the flour. Beat with whisk.

Add the sardines and their oil, then remove from the heat.

Break the egg into the cup, add salt and pepper and beat with a fork.

14

Pour the beaten egg into the pan. Mix well.

Pour the mixture back into the bowl to cool.

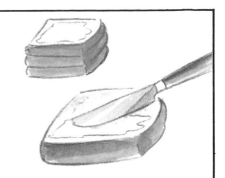

Spread 4 slices of bread with the mixture . . .

. . . and place the other 4 slices on top.

In the frying pan, gently heat the butter with a little oil so that it does not burn.

Fry the crispy sardine sandwiches for 5 minutes on each side. Serve hot.

...NOT BEATING!

15

CHEESE DIP
A LA PETITSUIX

SERVES 8 TO 10
Preparation: 40 mins
Equipment: colander, knife, fork, chopping board, bowl, large round serving dish.

INGREDIENTS

a cauliflower

a bunch of radishes

celery

bundle of carrots

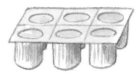

6 natural petits-suisses

100g Roquefort

100g double cream

2 tablespoons red wine vinegar

pepper salt

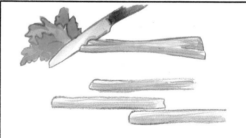

> IT'S RUDE TO SLOBBER OVER YOUR FOOD!

Separate the cauliflower florets and rinse.

Peel and wash the carrots. Cut them into pencil-thin strips.

Trim off the leaves and ends of the celery sticks. Wash and cut each stick into three widthwise.

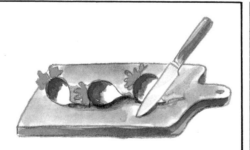

Top and tail the radishes keeping 2 cms of greenery. Wash them well.

In a bowl, mash the Roquefort with a fork.

Add: double cream, petits-suisses, vinegar and pepper. Mix well.

Taste the dip.
Add salt if necessary.

Place the dip in the middle of the serving dish. Arrange the vegetables around it.

Help yourself to vegetables and dip in!

INFAMUS EXOTIC SALAD

SERVES 4
Preparation: 20 mins
No cooking
Equipment: kitchen knife, chopping board, serving dish, glass, tin opener.

INGREDIENTS

small tin of hearts of palm

1 grapefruit

4 tomatoes

2 ripe avocadoes

1 lemon

100g black olives or raisins

lemon vinaigrette

IT'S EXOTIC SALAD TODAY. A RECIPE I BROUGHT BACK FROM ONE OF MY AFRICAN CAMPAIGNS.

Slice the tomatoes and arrange around the edge of the serving dish.

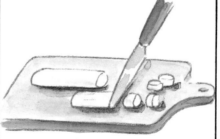

Set aside 2 whole hearts of palm. Slice up the others.

Decorate the centre of the dish with the whole and the sliced hearts of palm.

Cut the avocadoes into four. Remove the skins and the stones.

Immediately sprinkle with lemon juice to stop them going black.

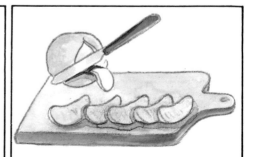

Peel the grapefruit. Remove the skin from each segment.

18

Place the grapefruit and the avocadoes between the tomatoes and the hearts of palm.

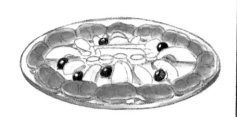

Garnish with olives. If you do not like olives, use raisins soaked in hot water until swollen.

Just before serving, pour vinaigrette over the salad.

INFAMUS, YOU'RE FAMOUS FOR YOUR FABULOUS FOREIGN FOOD.

WELL I'VE HAD MY CHANCES. JOIN THE LEGION AND SEE THE WORLD.

DRUID'S MARSHMALLOW SALAD

SERVES 4
Preparation: 30 mins **No cooking.**
Equipment: kitchen knife, bowl, chopping board, potato peeler, large salad bowl.

INGREDIENTS

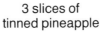

12 marshmallows

½ white cabbage

3 slices of tinned pineapple

1 green pepper

3 carrots

1 lemon

100g mayonnaise

2 tbsp double cream

salt and pepper

HEY, ASTERIX. DO YOU THINK GETAFIX WILL LET ME TASTE HIS MAGIC SALAD?

Remove any yellow outer leaves of the cabbage and rinse.

Cut the cabbage into fine strips.

Wash the green pepper.

Cut the green pepper into rings and remove any seeds.

Peel the carrots with the peeler and cut them into thin strips.

Drain the pineapple slices then chop them into cubes.

20

In a bowl, mix the lemon juice, double cream and mayonnaise. Season to taste.

Put the vegetables, marshmallows and pineapple in the salad bowl.

Just before serving, add the dressing and mix well. Season again, if necessary with salt and pepper.

?

ARE YOU GOING TO LET ME MAKE THIS SALAD OR NOT?

21

ORINJADE'S AVOCADO STUFFED TOMATOES

SERVES 4
Preparation: 15 mins
No cooking required
Equipment: kitchen knife, fork, colander, teaspoon, bowl, chopping board, grater, serving dish.

ORINJADE IS EXPECTING US FOR DINNER. SHE'S PREPARED HER SPECIALITY!

INGREDIENTS

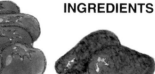

8 ripe but firm medium tomatoes

2 ripe medium avocadoes

1 lemon

1 green pepper

1 small onion

salt

2 tablespoons mayonnaise

Cut lids off the tomatoes. Reserve them. Spoon out the tomato flesh.

Salt lightly inside the tomatoes and place upside down in a colander.

Halve the avocadoes. Remove skins and stones. Place in a bowl.

Mash the avocadoes with a fork and cover with squeezed lemon juice.

Wash the green pepper, slice it then chop it into small cubes.

Peel the onion and chop it up as finely as possible . . .

22

. . . or, if you have one, use a grater.

Add the green pepper, the onion and mayonnaise to the mashed avocado. Mix.

Fill the tomato shells. Replace lids. Serve on a bed of lettuce.

I'D ADVOCATE YOUR AVOCADO STUFFED TOMATOES TO ANYONE ORINJADE!

23

GERGOVIAN MEAT BALLS

SERVES 4
Preparation: 20 mins **Cooking:** 40 mins
Equipment: bowl, mixing bowl, measuring jug, garlic press, fork, draining spoon, large pot, serving dish.

INGREDIENTS

500g minced beef

500g frozen peas or petits pois

60g fresh breadcrumbs

2 cloves garlic

one teaspoon nutmeg

2 tablespoons parsley

1 egg

salt

pepper

200ml water

50ml oil

THE SHECRET OF THISH RECHIPE ISH IN THE PARSHLEY!

Put the minced beef into the bowl.

In the large bowl, soak the breadcrumbs in hot water. Squeeze out by hand.

Add the breadcrumbs to the minced beef. Break an egg into the bowl.

Add the parsley, the nutmeg, salt and pepper.

Crush garlic cloves or with a garlic press, squeeze the 2 cloves of garlic onto the mixture.

Mix all the ingredients together with your hand or with a fork.

24

Make the meatballs by rolling the mince between your palms. Do not make them too big.

Pour the 200ml of water and the 50ml oil into a pan. Bring to the boil.

Plunge the meatballs one by one into the pan using a draining spoon.

Lower the heat. Simmer for 30 mins.

Add the frozen peas and cook for a further 10 mins.

Drain and arrange on a serving dish.

GLADIATOR'S SKEWERED SHRIMPS

GLADIATORS, NAME YOUR WEAPONS!

SERVES 4
Preparation: 15 mins **Cooking:** 20 mins
Equipment: 4 skewers, chopping board, kitchen knife, large pan, wooden spoon, gratin dish, (or/frying pan and garlic press), serving dish.
Preheat oven: Gas 8 (230°C)

INGREDIENTS

600g
large frozen
uncooked shrimps

2 onions

50g pine
kernels

50g flaked
almonds

50g
raisins

300g
long grain
rice

1 chicken
stock cube

2 tbsp
honey

100ml
oil

salt
pepper

Push the shrimps onto the 4 skewers, place on a gratin dish. Rub some oil over them.

Peel the onions; cut into two then chop finely.

Put the remaining oil and the onions in the pan.
Cook gently.

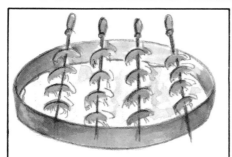

When the onions are transparent, add the rice and mix.

When the rice is transparent, add 1½ times its weight in water (450g).

Add the stock cube and honey. Cook gently, stirring often.

26

After 10 minutes add the pine kernels, almonds, raisins, salt and pepper.

Cook a further 10 mins. Taste. If the rice is tender, stop cooking. Turn off the heat.

Meanwhile, put the dish of shrimps under a hot grill, or in the oven at Gas 8. (230°C).

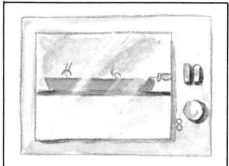

Grill the shrimps 5 minutes each side; or 10 minutes each side in the oven.

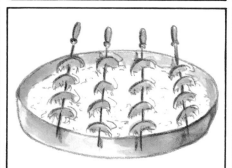

Arrange the rice in the serving dish and put the skewers on top.

Variation
The shrimps can be cooked in a frying pan with 2 tablespoons olive oil and 2 crushed garlic cloves.

IMPEDIMENTA'S CHICKEN DRUMSTICKS

OF COURSE, MY POSITION OF IMPORTANCE GIVES ME A CERTAIN AUTHORITY.....

Preparation: 10 mins **Cooking:** 1 hour
Equipment: Chopping board, kitchen knife, tablespoon, 2 ovenproof dishes, 1 pan, (or a microwave dish) 1 vegetable dish.
Preheat oven: Gas 4 (180°C)

INGREDIENTS

4 Chicken drumsticks

4 tbsps. French Mustard

8 thin slices smoked bacon

2 onions

200g double cream

salt and pepper

a large tin of petits pois

a large packet of plain potato crisps

Peel and halve the onions.	On the chopping board, cut them into rings.	Cover the bottom of the oven dish with the onion rings.	Spread each drumstick with a tablespoon of French mustard.

Season with salt and pepper. Wrap 2 slices of bacon around each drumstick.	Place the drumsticks on the onions. Cover them with double cream.	Put the dish into a pre-heated oven, Gas 4 (180°C) for 1 hour.

28

After 45 minutes, gently heat the petits pois in a pan for 15 minutes (or 6 minutes in a microwave oven).

When the chicken is cooked, heat the crisps in the second dish for 5 minutes in a moderate oven – Gas 2 (150°C).

IMPEDIMENTA, YOU SHOULD BE PROUD TO BE THE WIFE OF THE UNDISPUTED CHIEF OF THE VILLAGE, TO BE THE FIRST LADY, TO BASK IN MY REFLECTED GLORY....

STOP RABBITING ON AND HELP ME PLUCK THIS CHICKEN YOU OLD GOAT!

COMPANY'S CHEESE POTATO BAKE

SERVES 4
Preparation: 15 mins **Cooking:** 1 hour
Equipment: Potato peeler, kitchen knife, saucepan, colander, aluminium foil, earthenware or pyrex dish 24 cm in diameter.
Preheat oven: Gas 4 (180°C)

INGREDIENTS

800g potatoes	1 litre milk	400g double cream

2 cloves garlic	½ teaspoon of grated nutmeg	50g butter

salt   pepper

Peel the potatoes with the peeler and rinse.

Cut into slices 2mm thick and place into the pan.

Add the cold milk, salt and pepper to the potatoes. Heat.

Remove from the heat before the milk boils over. Drain the potatoes.

Halve the cloves of garlic. Rub them over the bottom and the sides of the dish.

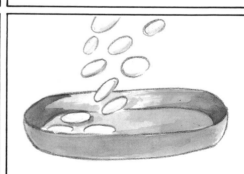

Arrange the potato slices in layers in the dish.

30

Mix nutmeg into the double cream. Season with salt and pepper. Pour over the potatoes.

Dot with flakes of butter to help with the browning. Put into the oven Gas 4 (180°C) for 1 hour.

If the potatoes brown too quickly, cover the dish with aluminium foil.

FAMOUS HAMBURGERS

INGREDIENTS

2 onions

600g lean minced beef

1 tablespoon Worcester sauce

1 tsp groundnut oil

50g butter

4 hamburger buns

salt   pepper

MAKES 4 HAMBURGERS
Preparation: 15 mins **Cooking:** 12 min
Equipment: Kitchen knife, chopping board, large bowl, frying pan, spatula.

YOUR HAMBURGERS ARE FAMOUS METALLURG? WHAT'S YOUR SECRET

With the knife, peel and halve the onions.

Place them on a board, flat side down. Cut them into 4 lengthwise.

Now slice them crosswise into small pieces.

Put the minced beef into the large bowl. Add the onions and Worcester sauce . . .

. . . salt and pepper. Mix well with (clean) hands and divide into 4 balls.

In the frying pan, melt the butter with the oil over moderate heat.

32

Place the meat balls in frying pan and gently flatten with the spatula.

Cook for about 5 minutes each side over a moderate heat.

Put the hamburgers in the halved buns and serve immediately.

QUITE SIMPLE ASTERIX, I PREPARE THEM WITH MY GOLDEN SICKLE!

SERVES 4
Preparation: 5 mins **Cooking:** 10 mins
Equipment: Large saucepan, kitchen knife, chopping board, frying pan with lid, wooden spoon.

DOGMATIX' HOT DOGS

INGREDIENTS

one french stick

4 frankfurter sausages

2 onions

2 tbsps oil

4 tbsps French mustard

WHAT'LL IT BE? IT'S ON THE HOUSE!

A HOT DOG FOR ME!

BARK BARK

HOT DOG

Heat water in a pot large enough to hold the frankfurters.

Pre-heat the oven to Gas 1 (140°C)

Peel the onions and halve them lengthwise.

Then chop each half into fine slivers.

Put both oil and onions into the frying pan, cover and cook gently for 10 minutes. Stir occasionally.

Cut the bread into four. Split open on one side.

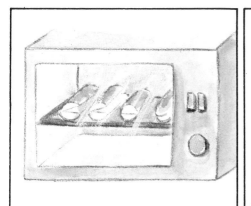

Warm the bread in the oven.

When the water boils, put the sausages in to cook.

After 10 mins. take the bread out of the oven.

When the sausages have cooked for 10 mins, take them out of the water.

Arrange the cooked onion inside the pieces of bread.

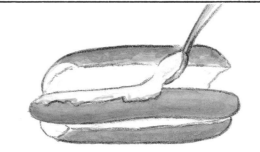

Add the sausages. Spread each sausage with mustard. Voila! Dogmatix Hot Dogs.

ANYONE TOUCHING MY DOG WILL BE DOG MEAT!

CORSICAN SMOKED CHICKEN RISOTTO

SERVES 4
Preparation: 30 mins **Cooking:** 20 mins
Equipment: Chopping board, kitchen knife, large pot, wooden spoon, measuring jug, serving dish.

AREN'T MY SMOKED CHICKENS READY YET?

INGREDIENTS

1 small tin tomato puree

2 onions

1 chicken stock cube

salt and pepper

100ml oil

300g American long grain rice

70g grated gruyere cheese

1 teaspoon mixed herbs

1 small smoked chicken or 500g smoked ham

Peel and halve the onions lengthwise.

Place them flat side down on the board. Slice thinly.

Chop into tiny pieces by slicing crosswise. Put into the pot with the oil.

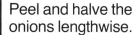

Pour 300g rice into a measuring jug.

Remove the chicken skin. Remove the meat from the bones and cut the meat into little pieces.
If using ham cut into small squares.

Over a moderate heat, cook the onions in the pot for 2 minutes. Add the rice.

36

Stir the rice until it has absorbed the oil and begun to brown.

In a measuring jug, measure a quantity of water equal to one and a half times the volume of rice. (450g)

Pour the water into the pot. Add the stock cube and the tomato puree. Stir. Lower the heat.

After 10 minutes, add the chicken or the ham, the mixed herbs, a pinch of salt and a little pepper.

Cook a further 10 minutes stirring often to prevent it from sticking to the pan.

Check if the rice is cooked. Add the grated cheese. Stir and transfer into the serving dish.

37

NORMAN SPAGHETTI SALMON

SERVES 4
Preparation: 15 mins **Cooking:** 10-12 mins
Equipment: Large pot, chopping board, colander, bowl, kitchen knife, wooden spoon, 4 plates.

INGREDIENTS

250g spaghetti

120g smoked salmon

butter

4 tablespoons double cream

100g grated parmesan cheese

1 tablespoon oil salt, pepper

HERE'S YOUR SPAGHETTI!

Bring a pot of water to the boil. Add oil and a pinch of salt.

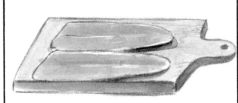

Remove the salmon slices from the packet and place on a board.

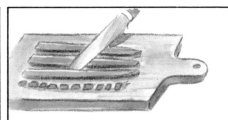

Cut into strips then into small pieces.

Put the spaghetti into the boiling water. Stir well. Cook for 10-12 minutes.

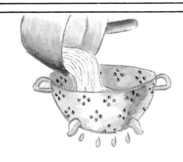

Test the spaghetti to see if it is cooked. Drain in a colander over the sink.

Put the pot back on the heat. Gently melt the butter. Add the spaghetti.

Mix well. Add the double cream.

. . . and the chopped salmon pieces. Add pepper. Mix. Remove from heat.

Serve the spaghetti straight onto the plates accompanied by a bowl of parmesan cheese.

THE BARD'S ROYAL BANANAS

INGREDIENTS

4 bananas

250g strawberries

1 punnet of raspberries

4 tablespoons redcurrant jelly

aerosol of cream

½ litre of vanilla ice cream

4 fan-shaped wafers

AS LONG AS HE'S EATING HE CAN'T SING!

Peel the bananas and cut into two lengthwise.

Put two banana halves onto each plate.

Wash strawberries in cold water.

Remove the green stalks. Dry the strawberries on kitchen paper.

Halve the strawberries and arrange them around the bananas.

Without washing them, place the raspberries between the bananas.

40

Put the redcurrant jelly in the bowl and whisk.

Put some jelly on each banana.

Take scoops out of the ice cream using an ice cream scoop or a tablespoon.

Arrange two balls of ice cream in the middle of each plate.

Shake the aerosol and decorate. Add a wafer.

Serve immediately before the ice cream melts.

NOW THAT I'VE FINISHED, I'LL SING YOU A LITTLE SOMETHING!

HUM?

OBELIX'S NUTTY BROWNIES

MAKES 16 BROWNIES
Preparation: 25 mins **Cooking:** 20-25 mins
Equipment: Frying pan, medium saucepan, mixing bowl, whisk, kitchen knife, non-stick baking tin 25 × 25 cm, chopping board, small piece aluminium foil, serving tray.
Pre-heat oven: Gas 4 (180°C).

INGREDIENTS

100g chocolate (65% cocoa)	2 eggs	150g sugar	100g plain flour

125g butter and 25g to butter tin	100g shelled walnuts	salt

Make a bain-marie by heating water in a frying pan.

Break the chocolate into squares. Put them into a saucepan with 125g of butter.

Stand the saucepan in the frying pan of boiling water. Keep stirring.

When the mixture is melted, turn off the heat.

Put the flour, sugar and eggs into the bowl.

Add a pinch of salt and beat with a whisk.

On the board, chop the nuts with a knife.

Add the nuts and the melted chocolate to the mixture in the bowl.

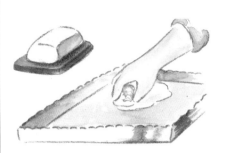

Butter the tin, holding the butter with the small piece of aluminium foil.

Pour the mixture into the tin. Put into pre-heated oven Gas 4 (180°C)

After 20 mins check the cake. The top should not be shiny. A knife put into the centre of the cake should come out moist.

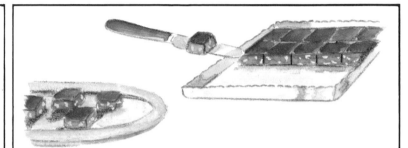

Take the cake out of the oven. Leave to cool in the tin. Cut into squares and place on a plate. The brownies can be served with vanilla ice cream.

VIKING'S ICE CREAM DREAMS

MAKES 4 ICE CREAM CUPS
Preparation: 10 mins
Cooking: 5 mins
Equipment: 4 deep glasses, medium saucepan, whisk, colander, kitchen knife, ice cream scoop.

INGREDIENTS

½ litre strawberry ice cream

1 packet of mini meringues

250g strawberries

aerosol of cream

6 tablespoons of redcurrant jelly

¡ICEBERG DEAD AHEAD!

Put the four glasses in the refrigerator so that they are quite cold.

Put the 6 tablespoons of redcurrant jelly and the same amount of water in the pan.

Heat and blend with a whisk. Cool the mixture, whisking occasionally.

Wash and drain the strawberries before removing their stalks.

In each glass, put 4 strawberries, (cut up the largest ones). Add 2 or 3 mini meringues.

Scoop out the ice cream and place 2 balls in each glass.

Pour the cooled redcurrant jelly over the ice cream.

Shake the aerosol. Top each glass with cream.

Decorate with remaining strawberries and meringues.

45

CLEOPATRA'S EXOTIC GATEAU

SERVES 6
Preparation: 15 mins **Cooking:** 30 mins
Equipment: colander, 2 small saucepans,
non-stick cake tin 24cm diameter.
mixing bowl, whisk, serving plate.
Pre-heat oven: to Gas 4 (180°C)

GAULS! THANK YOU FOR SERVICES RENDERED. TAKE THIS GATEAU FIT FOR A QUEEN AND CUT IT INTO THREE.

INGREDIENTS

1 tin of
10 pineapple
slices in syrup

4 tablespoons
golden syrup

100g
butter

3 eggs

100g
plain flour

1 tablespoon
Baking
powder

100g
granulated
sugar

pinch
of
salt

Put the 4 tablespoons
of golden syrup into the
cake tin.

Using the spoon, spread the
golden syrup over the base
and up the sides of the tin.

Open the tin of pineapple. Drain
in the colander over a saucepan
and keep the juice.

Halve all the slices bar one. Arrange
them around the edge of the tin.
Place the whole slice in the middle.

Put the sugar, flour,
baking powder and
salt into a bowl.

In the other saucepan, gently
melt the butter (or in a bowl,
cook for 1 minute in a
microwave oven)

Add the 3 eggs one by one to the sugar and flour mixture; then add the melted butter.

Whisk until the mixture is creamy.

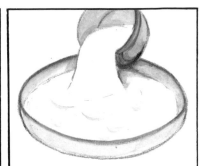

Pour into the cake tin. Bake on middle shelf of oven Gas 4 (180°C)

After 30 minutes take the gateau out of the oven and tip out onto a plate.

Gently heat the reserved pineapple juice in the saucepan for 10 minutes.

Pour the juice over the gateau. Allow to rest. Serve the gateau warm or cold.

SERVES 12
Preparation: 20 mins **Cooking:** 30 mins
Equipment: 2 bowls, 2 saucepans,
2 whisks, measuring jug, scales,
sieve, mixing bowl, electric whisk,
2 cake tins 24 cm diameter, frying pan,
serving plate, spatula,
Pre-heat oven. Gas 4 (180°C)

BELGIAN CHOCOLATE GATEAU

INGREDIENTS

300g
plain flour

300g
castor sugar

125g
butter

100g unsweetened
cocoa

200g
live yogurt

100g desiccated
coconut

200ml
hot water

1 teaspoon
powdered vanilla

1 teaspoon
bicarbonate of soda

1 teaspoon
salt

2 eggs

200g plain
chocolate

200g
double cream

aerosol of
cream

FOLLOW ME MY FRIENDS. COME AND TASTE MY SPECIALITY – BELGIAN GATEAU THERE ARE ONLY A FEW SLICES LEFT – JUST ENOUGH FOR A SNACK!

In a bowl, whisk together the cocoa and very hot water. Allow to cool.

Gently melt the butter in a saucepan or in a bowl, cook for one minute in a microwave oven.

In a mixing bowl, cream together the butter and sugar using a whisk.

Separate the eggs. Place the whites in a bowl and add the 2 yolks to the mixture in the mixing bowl. Whisk well.

Add the cocoa liquid, the sieved flour, the salt, the vanilla, the bicarbonate of soda and the yogurt. Mix well.

Beat the egg whites till stiff . . .

48

... fold gently into the chocolate mixture so as not to break down the air bubbles.

Butter 2 cake tins. Divide the mixture between them. Put in oven, Gas 4 (180°C) for 30 minutes. When cooked remove from oven and allow to cool.

Melt the plain chocolate in a saucepan standing in a hot water-filled frying pan. Away from the heat, add the double cream.

Tip out one cake onto the serving plate. Spread with ⅓ of the chocolate cream, sprinkle with coconut.

Tip the second cake onto the first. With a spatula, cover the top and sides with the remaining chocolate cream. Refrigerate.

Just before serving, decorate with aerosol whipped cream.

49

SERVES 4 – 6
Preparation: 15 mins
Cooking: 30 mins
Equipment: bowl, mixing bowl, 2 knives, earthenware or pyrex dish 28cms diameter, kitchen paper.
Pre-heat oven: Gas 9 (240°C)

LOVER'S APPLE CRUMBLE

INGREDIENTS

5 golden delicious apples

50g raisins
or
1 punnet of raspberries

150g plain flour

220g brown sugar

150g soft margarine

200g single or double cream

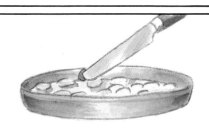

ARENT YOU GOING TO GIVE HER THE APPLE CRUMBLE THEN?

POM! POM! POM!

If using raisins, soak them in a bowl of hot water.

Put the flour and brown sugar into the mixing bowl.

Add the margarine cut into three pieces. With a knife in each hand . . .

. . . cut the margarine into the flour until it has the consistency of breadcrumbs.

Peel the 5 apples. Quarter and core them.

Cut the apple quarters into little pieces and put into an oven dish.

Drain the raisins, Dry them with kitchen paper.

Sprinkle the raisins (or the raspberries) onto the flan.

Pour the flour, margarine and sugar mixture over the apples. Bake in the bottom of the oven at Gas 9 (240°C).

After 10 minutes, lower the temperature to Gas 4 (180°C) and bake a further 20 minutes.

The crumble is cooked when apple juice bubbles up at the edges.

Serve the hot or warm crumble with single or double cream.

51

PIRATE'S DARK CHOCOLATE MOUSSE

SERVES 4
Make a minimum of 2 hours ahead.
Preparation: 30 mins **Cooking:** 15 mins
Equipment: frying pan, medium saucepan, cup, tablespoon, wooden spoon, mixing bowl, electric whisk, serving bowl, spatula.

INGREDIENTS

200g chocolate
(65% cocoa solids)

100g
butter

4 eggs

2 tablespoons
hot water

1 tablespoon
instant coffee
granules

salt

Heat some water in a frying pan to make a bain-marie.

Break the chocolate into the saucepan. Add the butter.

Dissolve the coffee granules in a cup with two tablespoons of hot water.

Pour the coffee over the chocolate and stand the saucepan in the water-filled frying pan.

Stir until it is creamy. Allow to cool for 10 minutes.

Separate the eggs, putting the whites in a bowl. Stir the yolks into the saucepan one at a time.

 Add a pinch of salt to the egg whites and whisk into stiff peaks.

 Pour the chocolate into the serving bowl and, bit by bit, add the egg whites with a spatula.

 Gently fold the egg whites into the chocolate. Refrigerate for 2 hours.

NEW WORLD PANCAKES

THESE NEW WORLD PANCAKES ARE...

HOW!

MAKES 18 PANCAKES
Preparation: 15 mins
Resting time: 2 hours
Cooking: 30 mins
Equipment: 2 mixing bowls, whisk, strainer, kitchen paper, non-stick pan 20cm in diameter or smaller, ladle, spatula.

INGREDIENTS

4 eggs

2 tablespoons baking powder

maple syrup

500g plain flour

½ teaspoon vanilla essence

2 tablespoons granulated sugar

½ teaspoon salt

¾ litre milk

butter for the pan

Put the flour and eggs into a bowl and whisk together.

Whisking all the time, trickle in the milk.

Add the sugar, baking powder, salt and vanilla.

Pass the batter through a strainer to remove any lumps. Leave to rest for 2 hours.

Using some kitchen paper, butter the pan. Heat over a moderate flame.

Carefully pour about ½ a ladle of batter into the pan to make a thickish pancake, 12 cms in diameter.

When the upper surface is dry and full of holes, turn over with a spatula.

Cook the other side for 2 minutes. Lift the edge to check if it is ready.

Pour maple syrup over the pancake and eat immediately.

A LIBERATING EXPERIENCE!

WILD BOAR CHOCOLATE TRUFFLES

MAKES 40 TRUFFLES
Preparation: 30 mins **Cooking:** 20 mins
Equipment: medium-sized saucepan, wooden spoon, 2 wide plates, small spoon, serving tray.

INGREDIENTS

400g tin sweetened condensed milk

20g butter

2 tablespoons drinking chocolate

one packet chocolate vermicelli

40 paper cases for sweets

i LOVE TRUFFLES, BUT NOT CHOCOLATE ONES!

SNIFF! SNIFF!

Put the butter, the milk and the drinking chocolate into the saucepan.

Heat gently, stirring with a wooden spoon until the mixture is smooth.

The mixture is ready when the chocolate lifts away from the edge of the pan with a spoon.

Pour the mixture into a dish and allow to cool.

Remove a spoonful of the chocolate mixture . . .

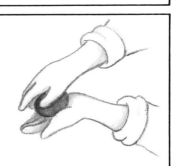

. . . and roll between your palms to form a small ball.

56

In the other dish, roll the balls in the vermicelli so that they are well covered.

Place the truffles into the paper cases and serve on a tray.

57

CAESAR'S IMPERIAL COCKTAIL

MAKES 4 LARGE GLASSES
Preparation: 10 mins
Equipment: 4 large glasses, jug, lemon juicer, 2 saucers, whisk, knife, chopping board.

INGREDIENTS

NOW THIS IS A DRINK FIT FOR CAESAR!

2 glasses (400ml) orange juice

1 glass of (200ml) pineapple juice

1 glass (200ml) grapefruit juice

3 tablespoons syrup of grenadine

1 orange

½ lemon

2 glasses (400ml) sparkling water

2 tablespoons castor sugar

Pour the orange juice, pineapple juice and grapefruit juice into the jug.

Add the syrup of grenadine and whisk.

Squeeze the ½ lemon and put the juice in a saucer.

Put the sugar into the other saucer.

Take a glass, dip the rim into the lemon juice . . .

. . . then into the sugar.

Frost the other 3 glasses in the same way. Allow to dry.

On the chopping board, cut 4 large slices from the middle of the orange.

With the knife, slit each slice from the middle to the edge.

Add the sparkling water to the jug and mix well.

Pour the cocktail into the 4 glasses. Add ice cubes.

Decorate each glass with a slice of orange.

I'LL LET CLEOPATRA TASTE SOME, SHE'S GOT A GOOD NOSE!

CRISMUS BONUS' MAGIC COCKTAIL

MAKES 4 LARGE GLASSES
Preparation: 10 mins
Equipment: jug, lemon juicer, 2 saucers, 4 large glasses, whisk, chopping board, kitchen knife.

HEE! HEE! WITH THE MAGIC COCKTAIL I PINCHED FROM THE GAULS, I'LL SEIZE CAESAR'S SEAT!

INGREDIENTS

2 glasses (400ml) pink grapefruit juice

1 (400ml) tin or 2 glasses of lemon soda (gini)

2 tablespoons of castor sugar

2 tablespoons syrup of citron

200ml pineapple juice

1 lemon

4 ice cubes

Pour the syrup of citron, the grapefruit and the pineapple juice into the jug. Whisk.

Wash the lemon under hot water.

Squeeze half the lemon and pour the juice into a saucer. Keep the other half.

Put the two tablespoons of sugar into the other saucer.

Take each glass in turn and dip the rims into the lemon juice, then into the sugar.

You now have frosted glasses.

Cut 4 slices from the other lemon half. Make a slit in each slice from the middle to the edge.

Add the soda to the jug and mix.

Pour the cocktail into the 4 glasses. Add an ice cube to each and decorate with a lemon slice.